Card MAGIC

Jon Day

Illustrated by
Chris Fisher

Contents

Kingfisher Books

All about card magic

This book shows you how to do ten great card tricks. On this page you can find out about some of the things you will need to become a good magician.

You don't have to dress up, but wearing a **cloak** and **hat** is fun and may help you give a better performance.

Pockets are useful for hiding cards in.

You can make a **magic wand** out of wooden dowelling. Paint it black and white.

You need a **table** to do many of the tricks on. Cover it with a **cloth** so the cards do not slide about while you are performing.

Some tricks require sticky tape, scissors, pencils, etc. There is a list of these things at the beginning of each trick.

Some special card words are explained in full on page 24.

The most important thing you need to be a good magician is **practice.**

Try the tricks out in private, doing them again and again until you can do them smoothly.

Try tricks out in front of a mirror to get an audience's eye view.

You need two identical packs of playing cards. One is your **performing pack.** The other is a **spare pack** which you use to make special trick cards.

If you have difficulty holding full-size cards, you can buy small-size packs.

Use all your **acting ability.** You have to persuade people that what they are seeing is magic! Knowing what to say, and how to say it, is as important as knowing how a trick works.

Hints

1 At the beginning of each trick, make sure you've got all the equipment ready and in the right place.

2 Never repeat a trick straight away, even when people beg you to do so. They will know just what to look for, and so may guess the secret of the trick.

3 Never show anyone how you did a trick. That is your secret as a magician!

Aces high

Things you need

Pack of cards

Get a friend to find all four Aces without trying.

Get ready . . .

Place the four Aces face down on top of the pack, but don't let anyone see you doing it.

Trick time

1 Tell a friend that he or she is going to do all the magic by finding the four Aces without even looking at the cards!

2 Ask them to pick up the pack and divide it into four piles of about the same size. **Make sure the pile with the Aces on top is in fourth place.**

This is the pile with the Aces on top.

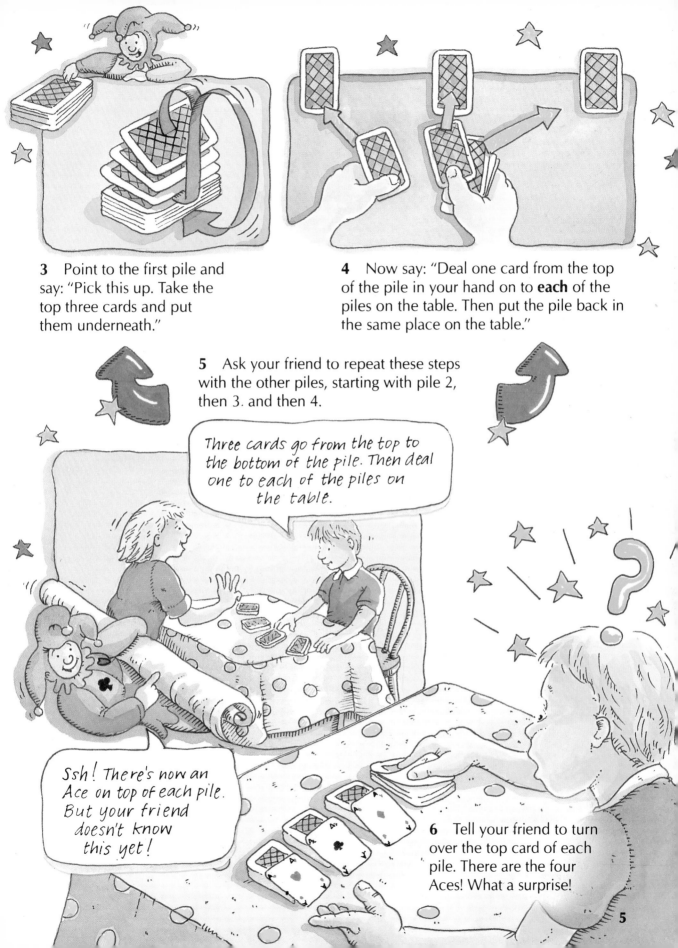

3 Point to the first pile and say: "Pick this up. Take the top three cards and put them underneath."

4 Now say: "Deal one card from the top of the pile in your hand on to **each** of the piles on the table. Then put the pile back in the same place on the table."

5 Ask your friend to repeat these steps with the other piles, starting with pile 2, then 3. and then 4.

Three cards go from the top to the bottom of the pile. Then deal one to each of the piles on the table.

Ssh! There's now an Ace on top of each pile. But your friend doesn't know this yet!

6 Tell your friend to turn over the top card of each pile. There are the four Aces! What a surprise!

The whispering cards

Astonish your friends by getting cards to talk to you!

Things you need

Pack of cards Pencil 12 identical envelopes

Get ready . . .

1 Take four of the envelopes and mark each one with a tiny pencil dot in the top **left**-hand corner of the flap.

2 Take another four and mark them with a dot in the top **right**-hand corner.

3 Leave the other four envelopes blank.

4 Stack all the envelopes in a pile in this order:

Left-dotted on top.
Right-dotted in the middle.
Blank underneath.

Trick time

1 Tell everyone that you can hear cards talking! You will be able to say whether a card is a Jack, Queen or King just by listening to it whispering to you!

2 Take the four Jacks, four Queens and four Kings from the pack. Put them in a pile with Jacks on top, then Queens, then Kings.

There's no need to seal the envelopes, but turn them over so nobody can see the dots.

3 Put a Jack in each of the top four envelopes, a Queen in the next four, and a King in the last four.

4 Give the envelopes to someone and ask them to mix them up on the table.

Left-hand dot = Jack

Right-hand dot = Queen

No dot = King

I can hear a young man's voice. He says his name is Jack!

5 Now pick one envelope from the table. Hold it up, looking casually for a dot on the back as you do so.

I can hear a woman's voice. It must be the Queen!

This one is a man's voice. It's the King!

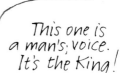

6 Now you begin acting! Hold the envelope to your ear and listen to it, as if you could hear a whisper inside. Say "Tell me who you are please." Tell your audience if it is a King, Queen or Jack inside. Make up your own script, or follow the one used here. Take out the card to see if you are right. (Of course you are!)

7 Repeat steps **5** and **6** with each of the envelopes. Everyone will be amazed!

Jumping Jack

Things you need

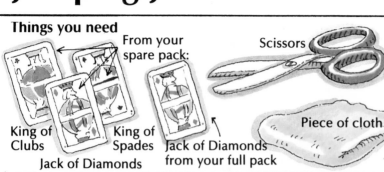

King of Clubs

King of Spades

Jack of Diamonds

From your spare pack:

Scissors

Jack of Diamonds from your full pack

Piece of cloth

Make the Jack jump out of your friend's hands and into your pocket!

Get ready . . .

25mm

20mm

Trim off 1.5mm

1 Cut a piece about this size out of one end of the spare Jack.

2 Make the two Kings slightly narrower by trimming off about 1.5mm from one edge of each.

3 Put the 'real' Jack of Diamonds in your pocket.

Trick time

You need to be seated at a table to do this trick.

Cut part hidden behind King.

Make sure the cut end is between their thumb and forefinger.

1 Hold the three cards like this, and show them to your friends.

2 Tell your friends you will make the Jack jump out of their hands into your pocket.

3 Close the cards and ask someone to hold them between their thumb and first finger.

4 Say: "In a minute this is what I'll do to make the Jack jump. I'll just show you."

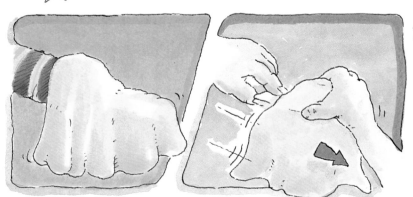

5 Drape the cloth over your friend's hand and quickly remove it again, **taking the Jack with you.** Do this by gripping the edges of the card and pulling. Only the Jack will move, and your friend will feel nothing.

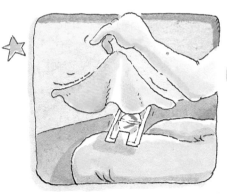

6 You have already done the trick, but nobody realizes! Drop the cloth and Jack in to your lap.

7 Say "Now I'm going to put the cloth over your hand and make the Jack jump out into my pocket."

8 Put the cloth over your friend's hand and 'steal' the Jack again.

9 Ask your friend to look for the Jack. It has gone!

10 Pull the (other) Jack from your pocket . . . proving it jumped as you said it would do!

The impossible card trick

Things you need

Pack of cards

Pencil

Find the card your friend chose without looking at the pack at all!

Get ready . . .

1   Choose any card and mark it lightly with pencil dots in the top-left and bottom-right corners.

This is called a **key card**. It will help you find any card your friend chooses.

Pencil dot

Pencil dot

26th card

2   Put your **key card** back into the pack **in the 26th position from the top.**

25 cards

key card is number 26

Trick time

This pile **must** be more than half the pack or the trick won't work.

Pile A

Pile B

Pile C

Your **key card** will now be in pile B.

1   Place the pack face down on the table (pile A).

2   Get a friend to lift off more than half the cards and place them on the right (pile B).

3   Now ask your friend to lift off 'about half' of pile B and put these cards on the right, making pile C.

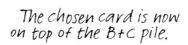

The chosen card is now on top of the B+C pile.

Pile B

Pile A

B+C pile

Point out that so far you have not touched the cards at all.

4 Point to pile C and say: "Pick this pile up and shuffle it. Look at the top card, remember it, and then put it back on top."

5 Then say: "Now put the cards (pile C) on top of this pile (pile B)."

6 Ask your friend to pick up pile A, shuffle it and put it on top of the B + C pile.

Make sure you can see the top left-hand corner of every card.

If this is card 1...

... then this is card 26.

If you get to the end of the row before reaching number 26, go back to the left-hand end and carry on counting.

7 Pick up the cards and spread them out on a cloth-covered table or carpet. Spread them from left to right, making them overlap.

8 Ask your friend to hold your wrist, so you can feel their vibrations! Move your finger over the cards, from left to right. When you see the pencil dot on the **key card,** count it (silently!) as 1. Carry on counting until you reach card 26, **which is your friend's chosen card.**

But that's impossible isn't it?

9 Don't pick the card out right away. Hover around it for a while, picking up the vibrations!

10 Pull out the card, still face down. Turn it over . . . **it's the card your friend chose!**

Circus trick

Pack of cards

Your friends will be so sure you've made a mistake they'll bet their money on it.

Get ready . . .

This simple trick was once used by circus and fairground entertainers to cheat people out of their money.

With practice, you will find it an easy trick to do. But don't take your friends' money – you're a magician, not a cheat!

Trick time

1   Ask a friend to shuffle the cards. As you take them back, sneak a look at the bottom card. Make sure you remember it – it's called the **key card.**

2   Spread the cards out between your hands. Ask the friend who shuffled to choose a card and remember what it is.

This is the key card.

Chosen card

Chosen card

Chosen card

Key card and chosen card

3   Gather the cards back together. Tell your friend to put their chosen card back on top of the pack.

4   Now cut the pack (see page 24 to find out how to do this). Your friend's card will move to the middle of the pack – and the **key card** will be right on top of it!

5 Hold the pack face down. Deal one card at a time, face up, in a line across the table.

Tell everyone you'll be able to pick out the chosen card just by feeling it. Pretend to feel each card carefully as you deal it out on to the table.

6 When you deal out the key card, **the next card you turn over will be the one your friend chose.**

Keep a straight face.

Chosen card

7 Deal out the chosen card, feeling it as before. Play-act a bit, taking your time and looking unsure.

8 Pretend to reject the card, then deal out three or four more. Look excited about the next card. Keep it in your hand and say: "I bet the next card I turn over will be the one you chose."

Ha Ha! The card I chose is already on the table.

9 It's clear the chosen card is already on the table. Your friend will be happy to take on the bet.

10 Everyone expects you to turn over the card in your hand, but you reach out to the chosen card **on the table** and turn it over!

You've done just what you said you'd do, and your friend has lost the bet.

The vanishing Queen

Things you need

Scissors

Make a Queen disappear and a Joker appear in her place!

From your spare pack:

A Queen **Two Aces** **A Joker**

Sticky tape

Get ready . . .

1 Cut out the centre section of the Queen card, keeping the head pieces from each end.

Cut out the centre bit (about one third of the card).

Make sure the sticky tape doesn't show on the other side.

2 Put the head pieces together, one facing up and one facing down. Join them together, as shown, making a hinge with sticky tape.

3 Fold up the hinged card, so the sticky tape is inside. Slide it over one end of the Joker. Now you are ready to begin.

Trick time

Practise this bit to get it right.

Hinged piece this end.

1 Place the trick card between two Aces. Hold them in one hand. Show them to your audience.

2 Close the cards by pushing them down with your finger.

3 Hold the cards face down. **Make sure the hinged edge is nearest to you.**

4 Pull out the bottom card and carefully place it face down on the table.

5 Put the next card (the Joker) down on the table. **Keep the hinged piece in your hand.**

6 Put the last card down. Move the cards about, asking everyone to watch the Queen.

Slip the hinged piece into your pocket now, while nobody's looking!

7 Ask someone to point to the card they think is the Queen. Turn the other two cards over slowly.

8 Now turn over the last card. Everyone thinks it's the Queen, but it's the Joker! She has vanished!

Oops!

Things you need

Glue

From your spare pack:
King of Hearts   Queen of Spades   Any other card   Pack of cards

Oops – your friends will think you've chosen the wrong card! But with a wave of your hand you change it to the right one.

Get ready . . .

Use the three spare cards to make a trick 'flap' card.

Glue

Glue

Fold the flap up, and the card is a king. Fold it down, and it's a Queen.

1 Fold the King and Queen carefully in half.

2 Glue two halves together, back to back.

3 Glue the other two halves to the **face** of the third card.

Flap card

Real Queen of Spades

Now you're going to ask a friend to choose a card – but you have to make sure it's the Queen of Spades.

4 Put the flap card on the bottom of your full pack. Make sure it shows the King. Take the **real** King of Hearts out of the pack. Place the **real** Queen of Spades on top of the pack.

16

Trick time

1 Get a friend to cut the pack in half. Pick up the **bottom** half and rest it on the top half, like this.

2 Now distract your friend by talking! Say "You could have cut the cards anywhere, couldn't you?"

3 Point to the cards and ask "And we've marked where you cut it like this?" Pick up the pile resting on top.

4 Point to the card on top of the other pile. Say "Look at the card you cut to, and remember it."

Of course, it is the Queen of Spades – the card that was on top of the pack in the first place!

5 Put the pack back together and ask your friend to put the chosen card into the middle.

6 Shuffle the cards and look at them, face up. Find the King of Hearts flap card and hold it up.

7 Try this script:

You: Is this the card you chose?
Friend: No.
You: Oops! Sorry. What was it?
Friend: The Queen of Spades.
You: Then watch!

8 Cover the King with your hand. 'Wipe' your hand over it, pulling the flap down. Suddenly the Queen appears!

Hypnotised cards

Things you need

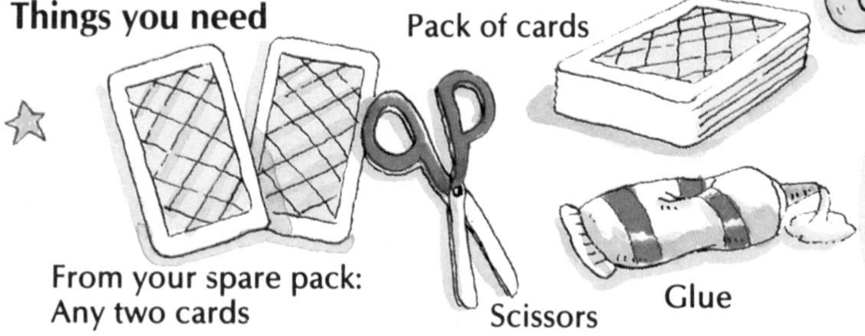

Pack of cards

From your spare pack:
Any two cards

Scissors

Glue

Make lots of cards hang suspended in the air, as if by magic!

Get ready . . .

1 Carefully cut a small flap in the centre of one card, as shown here.

2 Put glue on the face of the cut card and stick it to the back of the other.

You must be able to move the flap up and down.

Glue

Make the sides of the flap about 1cm long.

Be careful! Don't get glue on the flap area!

Fold the flap up along the dotted line.

3 When the glue is dry, place your trick flap card on the bottom of a pack of cards.

Put the flap card here. Make sure the flap is closed.

Trick time

1 Pick up the pack and slide off the flap card, secretly opening the flap as you do so.

2 Put the card face up on your hand so the flap goes down between your second and third fingers.

3 Grip the flap to hold the card steady. Then start slowly sliding cards into the gap between your palm and the flap card.

4 Press the first finger of your other hand on the cards to hold them steady. **Turn both hands over.**

5 Pretend to concentrate hard, then slowly remove the supporting finger. All the cards remain suspended, as if hypnotised!

6 After about 10 seconds, turn your hand over and let the cards fall on to the table. The flap will close and nobody will know how you did the trick.

The rising card

Things you need

Pack of cards

From your spare pack:
Any four cards

Scissors

About 10cm of
elastic thread
(shirring elastic)

or

a thin
rubber band

Glue

Make any card your
friend chooses rise
slowly out of the
pack!

Get ready . . .

1   Use the four cards from the spare pack
to make this trick equipment. First, cut
1cm-long snips in the top of two cards.

2   Cut a piece of elastic
thread about 10cm
long. Tie a
knot near
each end.

*The knots
should be about
7cm apart when
the elastic isn't
stretched.*

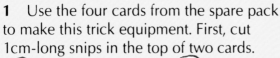

The best
elastic for this
trick is shirring
elastic – the kind
used on party hats and
masks. If you can't find
any, you could cut open
a thin rubber band and use
it instead.

knot

knot

3   Slip the elastic through
the slits in the cards, with
the knots at the back.

Glue
here

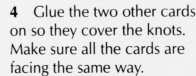

4   Glue the two other cards
on so they cover the knots.
Make sure all the cards are
facing the same way.

Trick time

Knots

Don't let them take the trick card!

1 Put the trick cards under the full pack, **with the elastic loop end toward you so you can see it.**

2 Spread the cards out face down between your hands and ask someone to choose one card.

Page 24 shows how to cut a pack of cards.

Put card in here.

3 Ask them to take the card, remember it, and put it face down on the table.

4 Cut the pack so the bottom half moves to the top and the trick cards move to the middle.

5 Pick up the chosen card and put it back into the pack, **into the elastic loop between the trick cards.**

Push it in to the loop.

6 Push the card in gently, making sure it goes into the loop and takes up the slack.

7 Grip the pack firmly and hold it up. Ask your friend to name the card they chose. **Gently** relax your grip. Their card will slowly rise from the pack like magic!

The knockout card trick

Things you need

A pack of cards

Pen

Small piece of paper

Guess what card your friend chose, and find its name inside your shoe!

Get ready . . .

1 Write this message on the paper.

2 Fold it up and put it in your right shoe.

You are thinking of the 8 of Hearts.

Put this message inside your shoe!

3 Find the 8 of Hearts and put it face down on top of the pack.

Now you must force your friend to choose the 8 of Hearts.

22

Trick time

1 Hold the pack behind your back, saying you can do this trick without looking.

Put the 8 of Hearts in here.

2 Slip the 8 of Hearts off the pack and on to the *back* of your hand. Cover it with the other hand.

The 8 of Hearts stays between your hands.

3 Turn your back on your friend. Ask them to take the pack, shuffle it, and put it back in your hands.

This step needs practice.

4 Turn to face your friend, sliding the 8 of Hearts back on top as you do so. Ask them to look at the top card, remember it, and put it back anywhere in the pack.

5 Look through the cards, trying to find the chosen one. Take out any card (except the 8 of Hearts). Without showing it, put it face down under your right foot.

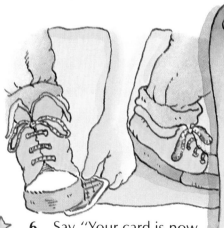

6 Say "Your card is now under my right foot." Pick up the card and show it.

7 Try this script:
You: Tell me, is this the card you chose?
Friend: No!
You (looking worried): Oh dear, can I try again?
Take off your shoe. Ask your friend to take the piece of paper out and read the message. It correctly names their card: the 8 of Hearts. Everyone will be KNOCKED OUT!

23

Card words

These are some special
words used in card magic.

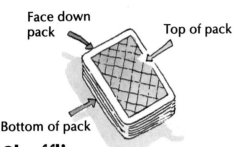

Face down pack

Top of pack

Bottom of pack

Face up pack

Face up card

Face down card

Shuffling

To shuffle is to change the order of all the
cards in a pack. There are different ways to
do this. You can hold the pack in one hand
and lift up some cards with the other. Put
the cards back into the pack, a few at a
time in different places, so the order of the
cards is changed. Repeat this until all the
cards have changed places.

Shuffling

Cutting

Cutting

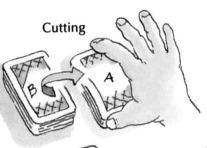

1 Cutting is a simple
way of changing the
order of cards in a
pack. Take some of the
cards (A) off the top of
the pack and put them
down to one side.

2 To complete the cut,
pick up the bottom half of
the pack (B) and put it on
top of the rest (A).

Produced for Kingfisher Books by
Times Four Publishing Ltd

Kingfisher Books, Grisewood & Dempsey Ltd, Elsley House,
24-30 Great Titchfield St, London W1P 7AD

First published in 1991 by Kingfisher Books

Typeset by C-Type, Horley, Surrey
Colour separations by RCS Graphics Ltd
Printed in

BRITISH LIBRARY CATALOGUING IN PUBLICATION DATA

Day, Jon
   Let's make card magic.
   1. Card tricks. Manuals
   I. Title   II. Fisher, Chris
   795.8   795.438

ISBN 0-86272-715-4